The World So Often

Luis García Montero (Granada, 1958) is one of the most read and influential Spanish writers today. He is an essayist, fiction writer, journalist, professor of Spanish Literature at the University of Granada, and, principally, a poet. He has received numerous important honors, like the National Poetry Prize (1994) and the National Critic's Prize (2003), both in Spain, and the Poets of the Latin World Prize (2010), in Mexico. He has published eleven books of poetry, represented in *The World So Often*, his first anthology in English.

The World So Often
Poems 1982–2008

LUIS GARCÍA MONTERO

Translated by
KATHERINE M. HEDEEN
and VÍCTOR RODRÍGUEZ NÚÑEZ

CROMER

PUBLISHED BY SALT
12 Norwich Road, Cromer NR27 0AX, United Kingdom

All rights reserved

© Luis García Montero 2013
English translations and introduction
© Katherine M. Hedeen and Víctor Rodríguez-Núñez 2013

The right of Luis García Montero to be identified as the
author of this work has been asserted by him in accordance
with Section 77 of the Copyright, Designs and Patents Act 1988.

This book is in copyright. Subject to statutory exception
and to provisions of relevant collective licensing agreements,
no reproduction of any part may take place without the written
permission of Salt Publishing.

Salt Publishing 2013

Printed and bound in the United States by Lightning Source Inc.

Typeset in Swift 9.5 / 13

*This book is sold subject to the conditions that it shall not,
by way of trade or otherwise, be lent, re-sold, hired out,
or otherwise circulated without the publisher's prior consent
in any form of binding or cover other than that in which
it is published and without a similar condition including this
condition being imposed on the subsequent purchaser.*

ISBN 978 1 84471 903 7 paperback

The World So Often: Poems 1982–2008 by Luis García Montero, selected, introduced and
translated into English by Katherine M. Hedeen and Víctor Rodríguez Núñez, has been
published with a subsidy from the Ministry of Education, Culture and Sport of Spain.

*Tantas veces el mundo: Poemas 1982–2008 de Luis García Montero, obra seleccionada,
prologada y traducida al inglés por Katherine M. Hedeen y Víctor Rodríguez Núñez, ha sido
publicada con una subvención del Ministerio de Educación, Cultura y Deporte de España.*

1 3 5 7 9 8 6 4 2

Contents

Acknowledgements ix
Luis García Montero, the Poetry of Experience and Something More xi

FROM *Tristia*
  The Cars 3
  Homage 5
  The Scene of the Crime 7

FROM *Foreign Garden*
  To Name Us (1941) 11
  Like Each Morning 13
  To Federico, with Some Violets 15

FROM *Complicit Journal*
  Invitation 21
  First Book 24
    III 24
    V 25
    XI 27
    XV 28
    XX 29
    XXV 30
  Second Book 31
    XV 31
    XVIII 32
    XIX 33
    XXVI 34
    XXVIII 35
  Invitation to Return 36

FROM *The Flowers of Cold*

   Crossed-Out Song   41
   Bitter Song   42
   Song with No One   43
   Song of Mist   44
   Evicted Song   45
   Night Song   47
   Verlaine Song   48
   Furniture Store   49
   Loose Adaptation of Immortality   52
   Nocturne   54

FROM *Separate Rooms*

   The Traveler's Reasons   59
   The Mirrors   61
   First Day of Vacation   62
   The World So Often   64
   The Insomnia of Jovellanos   66

FROM *Completely Friday*

   Monday Man with a Secret   71
   Confessions   74
   August's City   75
   Doubtful Urban Geography   76
   Tuesday and Literature   78
   Saturday Night Crime   80
   Impossible Song   82
   The City   83
   The Car   85
   Immortality   88

The Night	90
The Past	92
Poetry	94
Politics	95
Old Age	98

FROM *Inner Life of the Snake*

On Turning Forty	103
Corner 40 Song	106
Sun Song	107
Waiting Song	108
2001 Song	109
Pornographic Song	110
New Year's Eve (1940, 1970, 2000)	111

FROM *Eyestrain*

Hometown	119
One Language	121
First Verses	123
New York	124
The Professor	125
Children	127
Market Memories	129
Anniversary (2004)	131
Memory of Happiness (A Beach in Rota)	132
My Future and Heraclitus	134
Prints	135

Translator Notes	137

Acknowledgements

The translators wish to thank Luis García Montero for his support and patience. We are also grateful to the Ministry of Education, Culture and Sport of Spain for generously funding this project.

Luis García Montero, the Poetry of Experience and Something More

Luis García Montero (Granada, 1958), one of the most read and influential Spanish writers today, sees himself as "a poet of experience" (9). According to his own definition, this poetry is not content with giving "superficial accounts of life," but rather, on the contrary, attempting "to create artistically, thanks to sentimental perspectivism, the necessary conditions for reproducing in the reader the aesthetic experiences lived by the poet" (10). It distances itself from "the excessive intellectualism and experimental diversion" (10), which, in his view, prevailed in Spanish verse in the seventies, and returns to "the traditions of moral reflection and aesthetic realism" (11) that, also according to him, distinguished the poetic production immediately prior. This poetry certainly rejects the work of the group of Spanish poets from the seventies known as the *novísimos*—such as Pere Gimferrer, Guillermo Carnero, Ana María Moix and Leopoldo María Panero—to affirm the work of their predecessors, "Jaime Gil de Biedma and other members of his generation"—José Manuel Caballero Bonald, Antonio Gamoneda, José Agustín Goytisolo, Claudio Rodríguez, José Ángel Valente, among others—the so-called *Generación del 50* [50s Generation] (10). Dialectical negation and affirmation, like in all admirable art, arrives at a synthesis, a different condition.

García Montero is a poet, essayist, fiction writer, journalist and professor of Spanish Literature at the University of Granada. Among his books of essays, particularly worthy of mention are *Poesía, cuartel de invierno* (1987, 1988 and 2002), *El realismo singular* (1993), *Aguas territoriales* (1996), *El sexto día: Historia íntima de la poesía española* (2000), *Gigante y extraño: Las Rimas de Gustavo Adolfo Bécquer* (2001), *Los dueños del vacío* (2006) and *Inquietudes bárbaras* (2008). He is the author of the short story collection entitled *Luna del sur* (1992) and the novels *Mañana no será lo que Dios quiera* (2009) and *No me cuentes tu vida* (2012). He has worked as a columnist for the newspaper *Público* and has collected his articles in books like *La puerta de la calle* (1997), *La casa del jacobino* (2003) and *Una forma de resistencia* (2012). Still, above all, García Montero is a poet with numerous, important honors, like the National Poetry Prize (1994) and the National Critic's Prize (2003), both in his own country, and the Poets of the Latin World Prize (2010) in Mexico. He has eleven books of poetry, beginning with *Y ahora ya eres dueño del Puente de Brooklyn* (1980) up until his latest entry *Un invierno propio* (2012).[1]

Luis García Montero's poetry has commonly been considered—even by the author himself—as realist, yet this is a misinterpretation. The Nobel Prize winning poet, Octavio Paz, was among the first to recognize the focus of these poems on "exploring everyday reality, which, on the one hand, borders the marvelous and, on the other, the quotidian" (141). To this vision of reality open to the imagination it would be essential to add that, according to another major Mexican poet, Marco Antonio Campos, we are before the poetry "of a realist who expects too much from his dreams, and at the same time, of a dreamer who doesn't know, or at least doesn't think he knows how to experience reality very well" (95). Gabriele Morelli points out that here "reality and meta-reality come together, creating a dual space that embraces both art and life" (49). In other words, García Montero's search for "a *porous* writing that allows reality to penetrate the poems," where the poetic subject faithfully stands by "the truth of his experience" (González 21), doesn't necessarily imply an affiliation with realism. The resolve to represent reality truthfully is unquestionably present, but it is not the exclusive domain of 19th century aesthetics, which came to be in the last century the one and only revolutionary method of artistic creation.

---

1   Books available only in Spanish retain their original titles. The two poetry collections mentioned here, and a third, *Además* (Madrid: Hiperión, 1994), are not part of the present selection. For more information, see the website, www.luisgarciamontero.com.

In Luis García Montero's poetry, what we find is the device used by Bertolt Brecht in his transformative epic theater precisely to counteract realism: the distancing effect. And so he offers us, according to Pere Ballart, "a new, defamiliarized world where objects tell us all their misfortunes and illusions, which undoubtedly run parallel to our own" (24). The poetic subject doesn't try to trap the reader in an illusory world offered up as natural, but rather to break with the automatic perception of things and facts, and so avoid catharsis. In other words, this poetry proposes we not only focus on the signified, and thus it doesn't try to hide the signifier from us. As García Montero himself points out, it is true the poet of experience "doesn't invent a new language, instead he pledges to personally re-elaborate words intent on maintaining their appearance of second-hand material, their civic condition" (23). Still, we must keep in mind that—as Francisco Morales Lomas warns—here "prosaism" is toned down with the use of metaphor (42), and the poetic work reaches a "clearly avant-garde, experimental perspective" (43). Likewise, Laureano Lorenzo Ares adds that in the discourse of our poet words are "always laden with multiple meanings" (74), and for Antonio Jiménez Millán, "the writing of poems and the reflection on the meaning of poetry go hand in hand" (54).

The fact that Luis García Montero seeks to "abandon experimentalism" (13–14) and breaks with "art as the rupture of language" (15–16), does not imply the abandonment of or the breaking with experimentation and the awareness of language. In his poetry, what is crucial is precisely the use of a language that does not try to be transparent, a simple instrument of communication, and that risks its neck to be noticed. It's a language that is both reflection and matter, and thus, it has the agency to change things, the capacity to transform. For our poet, "it was necessary to restore the dignity language finds in the town square, in its ties to the social, as a shared space" (24). Moreover, this language is not limited to the lyrical tradition, it is open to lexicons marginalized for any number of reasons, it goes down to the streets and enters the classroom, it doesn't discriminate against words in any way, it becomes democratized. It combines prosaism and tropological density in search of a discourse with a greater power of representation and participation. As Jiménez Millán shows, in García Montero's verse there is ultimately an attempt to "defend language's ability to establish a dialogue with ourselves and with the other, to tackle literary fiction as a force of consciousness, of engaged individuality" (56).

García Montero's poetry not only distances itself from Realism but also from Romanticism and Symbolism, even their contemporary recurrences. Ernesto Che Guevara warned that "[t]he realistic art of the 19th century [. . .] also has a class character, more purely capitalist perhaps than the decadent art of the 20th century that reveals the anguish of the alienated individual." Despite opting for rationality—our poet states "if one can't believe optimistically in Reason [. . .] the outcomes of irrationalism aren't very positive either" (15–16)—there is a space in his verses for emotion, and especially for the anguish inseparable from modernity, referenced by Guevara. Joan Margarit has addressed García Montero in these terms, "[a] poet like you clearly understands that at the heart of all great problems there is always feeling. From this [. . .] poetry takes all its strength" (12). Yet in this aspect the poet's work also achieves a balance, at the same time there is sentimental rigor and intellectual outpouring. If, on the contrary, there were an absolute emotional identification with the lyrical speaker, the reader would lose the possibility to reflect in a critical, objective way. The end result is, as Laureano Lorenzo Ares states, "a fundamentally meditative poetry" (74).

Where García Montero's poetry truly surpasses "the poetry of experience" is in its rejection of solipsism. Here, "the suffering, deified romantic hero, in its *modernista*[2] and avant-garde manifestations" is left behind (García Montero 24), and yet, fortunately, neither the "option of individualism" (García Montero 12) nor "the

---

2   *Modernismo* refers to the influential Spanish American literary movement of the late 19th and early 20th centuries. It stems from a reaction against literary naturalism and bourgeois conformity and materialism. In general terms, it is characterized by innovation of literary form and an openness to diverse, "exotic" cultures.

reprivatization of literature" (García Montero 13–14) is reached. The poetic subject is far from being that "self-absorbed I, changed to an ivory tower or stable, more and more distanced from reality, less able to intervene in something that isn't a trend imposed by the same thing he denounces: the market" (García Montero 15–16). Rather, what is attained is "the fictionalization of the I, the urban word and the moral knowledge of individual consciousness" (García Montero 16). Thus, "poetry becomes a way to defend individuality from just one way of thinking and an exercise in consciousness" (Jiménez Millán 55–56). In other words, García Montero moves beyond "the poetry of experience" and goes ever deeper into dialogical poetry, which confronts the universal subject of knowledge, the self-sufficient I, the basis of modern dehumanization. It implies an active reader, a participant in the creation of the poem, which is always a collective work.

The present anthology has the goal of bringing the English-language reader up to date with regard to some of the most popular, crucial poetic work in the Spanish language today. As Angel González, an essential figure of the *Generación del 50*, recognized early on, Luis García Montero is "one of the most personal, important voices in new Spanish poetry" (21). And, later on, as Javier Bozalongo, one of the best poets of the most recent generation confirms, in this poetry "we saw ourselves and [. . .] we saw what we wanted to read and in many cases what we wanted to write" (77). The selection includes poems from *Tristia* [Tristia] (Melilla: Rusadir, 1982; Madrid: Hiperión, 1989), *El jardín extranjero* [Foreign Garden] (Madrid: Adonais, 1983; Madrid: Hiperión, 1989), *Diario cómplice* [Complicit Journal] (Madrid: Hiperión, 1987), *Las flores del frío* [The Flowers of Cold] (Madrid: Hiperión, 1991), *Habitaciones separadas* [Separate Rooms] (Madrid: Visor, 1994), *Completamente viernes* [Completely Friday] (Barcelona: Tusquets, 1998), *La intimidad de la serpiente* [Inner Life of the Snake] (Barcelona: Tusquets, 2003) and *Vista cansada* [Eyestrain] (Madrid: Visor, 2008). The collections that serve as sources are *Poemas* (Madrid: Visor, 2004) and *Vista cansada* (Madrid: Visor, 2008). Here then, dressed to the nines from head to toe, is the captain of "the poetry of experience" in Spain, whose poetic subject more often than not slips through his fingers, setting its own course to port in the always open, stormy waters of poetry.

KATHERINE M. HEDEEN and VÍCTOR RODRÍGUEZ NÚÑEZ

GAMBIER, MAY 1, 2013

Works Cited

Ares, Laureano Lorenzo. "El 'pulso' narrativo de la poesía de Luis García Montero." *EntreRíos* [Granada, Spain] 17–18 (Otoño-Invierno 2012): 70–75.
Ballart, Pere. "El código García Montero." *EntreRíos* 22–25.
Bozalongo, Javier. "Ciudades compartidas." *EntreRíos* 77–79.
Campos, Marco Antonio. "Queríamos un mundo distinto." *EntreRíos* 95–98.
García Montero, Luis. *Poemas*. Madrid: Visor, 2004.
González, Ángel. "*Completamente viernes*." *EntreRíos* 21.
Guevara, Ernesto Che. "Socialism and Man in Cuba". Translated by Aleida March. *The Che Reader*. North Melboren: Ocean Press, 2005. In *Marxist Internet Archive*. http://www.marxists.org/archive/guevara/1965/03/man-socialism.htm
Jiménez Millán, Antonio. "Luis García Montero: El diálogo y la conciencia". *EntreRíos* 54–56.
Margarit, Joan. "Carta a Luis García Montero". *EntreRíos* 10–12.
Morales Lomas, Francisco. "Aquel año 1998 y *Completamente viernes*". *EntreRíos* 41–44.
Morelli, Gabriele. "Metapoesía en Poemas de Luis García Montero". *EntreRíos* 47–50.
Paz, Octavio. "*Habitaciones separadas*". *EntreRíos* 141.

From *Tristia*

The Cars

The cars arrived suddenly one year
and time along with them. It was around nineteen
fifty-eight then.
The same linden trees still border the yard,
the same eyes from behind the window,
always monkish
facing the empty fountains of winter.
Out of the blue
life and its little things gave us love,
tiny cupboards to lock away our childhood.
Do you remember?
The rooftop was white, in the daytime doves
still land there.
Eyes watching us like a late-night fire
every time we run away from home.
I've searched for her skin in all my lovers,
the blonde swell of her shoulders,
the almond form overflowing from her mouth.
Later she'd place it in his hands,
the one who'd been there,
between us too,
like a soldier leaden, colossal.

Then I wonder if this face is mine
or if it's the old passion of a lost war.
Two minutes left before going on stage.
To feel how the lights sear
your neckline: sing,
sing for Paris
and for Siena,
you, the one who thinks time isn't a question
of linden trees or doves,
my lead soldier, old, wounded.
Close your sweet heart ill-spent
on park snows,

as if dawn had broken and you'd opened the window
to notice for the first time
winter had changed
to success.

Homage

You're surrounded by only a few things now.
Maybe you think you're immortal
on this night in the world,
when your body still hasn't chosen
to believe in history.
And you're sad,
—five years of keeping a silent eye on me—
gazing out solemnly from a photo.

(That evening you were
the lovely shadow of life.
You'll recall your mouth's hesitant move
when they surprised you. The bashful smile
I loved so many nights
now scares me off.
I'm not sure if it was the alcohol that made you beautiful,
if time imagined the champagne
wounded by your lips,
when you merely asked for the passion of a truce.

Just then
the future betrayed you. What's so insistent,
interrogating now, wasn't so fleeting before.
As if you'd known
I'd be sleepless years later,
needy in your presence).

You're remembered by some
for defending your legs from a light wind's boldness,
but all I want is your paper lips,
fair-haired heart dangling from the wall,
never to understand
your suicide very well.

Here
being isn't daily or fair.
Kiss me. Come back to life
if you can.

The Scene of the Crime

Past the shadows
your eyes give you away,
and I can tell you're smooth
like an open map
of fear and desire.
Give yourself up for dead
sweetheart,
it's a holdup.
Your lips or your life.

From *Foreign Garden*

To Name Us (1941)

How difficult it's getting to wake up together
                                    ÁLVARO SALVADOR

Only later they'd realize
both had sought a story
not so near love.
Maybe some excuse
to watch January trees
trembling above the park,
cross the lanes
of a city taken by hymns
and winter clothing
or find themselves with high hopes, accompanied
in the celestial glass of shop displays.

Perhaps it was just the times
that made it likely
for an old soldier of every defeat
to kill loneliness in the arms
of a young revue singer.

And they were tough times.
While rooftops
reclaimed their stench of filthy cats,
they
crossed the uniform-clad city,
endured the martial step of arrogance,
traveled the streets among calashes,
patient, broken,
searching for a room.

Only rain leaves
a faulty passion
on the lovers' empty bench,

only rains forgets
patent leather lies on the streets
and a diminutive love on each corner
for lips learning their song.

Maybe too
it was the switch to a counterattack,
feigning happiness,
not truly in love
at midwinter,
saying it doesn't matter since we're still alive,
since your eyes are here despite the smoke,
made for love, hardened by history,
filled with joy always at whatever cost.

A brief time later,
when the blind breeze of 1960
forced them to realize they'd aged,
they understood it was lovely to grow dark together,
embrace beneath any flag,
live the closeness imposed by defeat
not so near love,
since life as faithful
as an alluring melody
always ended up admitting they were right.

Like Each Morning

Now I know
these streets have made us lonesome
and our hearts
have the yellow pulse
of a trolley's sluggish woods.

Over their old bodies
we took slow, uneven steps
with a levelness like trees.

It was lovely to arrive
each morning,
honor our meeting with
the ivy on the wall,
tired draperies of narrow houses
and dirty streets. Lovely
to cross some bridge,
linger just long enough
to see water quarreling at the river's edge.

In its garden we sensed
the first winters, their hazy course
among the palms.
Almost no one went by,
there were only
forty red chairs
from closed bars and a perfect
loneliness.

For many years,
so many days gone by
one after the other,
our duty was a certain solitary stroll,
a date with a course we only altered
to trample the hours falling,

the dreams lacking,
puddles' frozen surface,
to jump the hedges
or kiss our nails purple with cold.
And when we arrived at the door we'd buy
little cream or violet candies.

We'd finally enter to mingle
like every morning in life
with tired steps, cold tiles
of a world fashioned in Latin
and Roman numerals.

Now I know
in that deserted city
everyone felt sorrow,
a perfect solitude
overflowing with long coats and umbrellas.

To Federico, with Some Violets

To Juan Carlos Rodríguez

Still some violets
Cannot weigh upon this shadow
And it's pleasant to leave them there
Fresh among the mist . . .

              LUIS CERNUDA

I

You're here once more. I waited for you
to offer a lost arm in the haze,
the bend of docks, the solitude of others
at Columbia University
and this cold ash
in the torn eyelids
of a sleepless city.

Now imagine
that weary sky,
those eyes of yours
from nineteen twenty-seven,
by then gone astray,
crossing bridges
like limitless motion.

In this South
of lights and trusses
death might arrive one morning,
but it's strange,
the experience of millennial love
history carries between its thighs,
patient, savage love
against us all.

Now imagine
the scaffolding,

an empty room and lust
sunken like a ship
in search of suicide.

You're in Harlem,
beneath the deaf noise of engines
you'll go silent,
alone with your sweat, your fear,
to see how it closes death's eyes,
how it kisses the lips of its last lover.

It was nineteen twenty-nine.
It shouldn't have been strange,
because after all you were there,
above life's murky sewers.

II

and remember a sad breeze in the olive groves
F. G. L.

After
the tired rush of the last trains
nothing returns. Just your
face lingering on Broadway,
and there's so much loneliness it's hard
to close my eyes and not doubt you exist.

Absurd
this fire language splitting the horizon,
untamable, spreading over our hearts,
multiform, wounded,
bursting, seeming
the forced smile of a broken mask.

Alone
the city disguised in shiver
and its eyes point to you
outlined, sightless
like a trace of teeth forgotten on shoulders.

Then
alcohol is blood undressing lips,
since night comes,
since death arrives on an arm
to leave you behind with your years.

Sad in the olive groves,
while Harlem windows stand ajar,
time is a breeze no one remembers now.

III

Here
after so many years and a war,
everything's like it was then.
In the boozy voice of the times
the schedule's the same, tired embraces
still arrive late
and life grieves
like a blow of mist hidden in your hands.

Our eyes
waiting to be laid out
over nineteen seventeen
hearts in place.
Now you see, just to tell you
life's possible, it's waiting for me
like an open wound over another waterway,

to rise beneath the numbers,
break solitude down, take the streets
and put dates in place.

Today a bunch of violets won't weigh
upon this shadow,
and it's sweet to leave them there
fresh in the mist
with an unending murmur of bodies
and this strange teardrop
we call history.

From *Complicit Journal*

Invitation

A long sea spit
lacking calm in the glance of a return,
this lane inhabits its loneliness with leaves,
tangles in the light like a cluster
of shadows or clay,
damp newspapers
over the indigo oil of tiles,
forgotten carmine on walls,
doubtful gardens
or ivy
engulfing the front gate's bourgeois irons.

Long sea spit in my memory.

Beneath the French light are refashioned
the lookout numbers on doorways,
the small Siren reflected,
her lips above the water,
the theater cleared of musicians
waiting for Sunday.
All of it like a primitive claim,
air raising heart's
head and pushing
toward the strange craft of writing its nostalgia.

Nothing's neutral,
not even the shadows of old houses
inquiring about
their lost landscapes on sidewalks,
not even the crane,
distant,
beautiful like a swan,
spreading its long neck to rest it
on the gray eaves of the horizon.

I went down to the city
at that doubtful,
foreseen hour
when all the traffic lights twinkle,
in the dark, drawn
field,
where the breeze of taxis blows
with its moss reflection,
where light veils
the brilliant bags beneath neighborhood eyes,
casting on each body
a long look, an empty scene.
I was in the city,
downhearted while crossing its signs,
wanderer in the glow of shop windows.
I want to turn the corner,
discover another back,
find a friendly, municipal heart
to open the door of its eyes for me
and let me in.

Call me,
I'll return with you,
slowly walking the no longer existent streets
when you don't call,
walking down you
in evening's slight rage.
Call me,
it's scarcely eight, scarcely a gentle
resonance of life
returns to the sidewalks,
muddled in the flash of teenagers,
takes rushed steps past the last stores,
opens it metallic,
human colors

of couples embracing in cars,
strangers glancing at one another
under the hesitant canvas of desire,
under the artificial moon.

Watch me return
beyond the tall houses of this distracted April,
me, the one who dreaded borders.

Amid the trees,
the sun looks like a drunkard's eye.

Call me,
today's another timetable,
the distinct heat of its sway,
image of servants with different blood,
the dignity of rational beings,
thinking hearts who could speak
if they weren't alone,
if someone called them.

Still everything orders your presence:
watch me return.

Open doorways,
billboards
remind me of your skin,
that doubtless realm
where I struggle to speak of the horizon.

The horizon
like the dirty bar in some strange tavern
where I'll never be able to lean.

First Book

III

Like the first cigarette,
the first embraces. A tiny
paper star
glowed on your cheek.
You took up the margins
where parties joined loneliness, music
or the gentle desire of a shared return,
almost always later.

Our possible, outlaw shadows
smoking, collars upturned,
didn't cross the darkness,
but those hours
becoming streets in public sets
for private love.
Talking silhouettes,
shadows where the history
of what we truly are now took shape,
once we wagered the stillness of our hearts.

Even the furniture
got used to us.
Facing the window—impossible to close—
in a room like ours,
with identical books and bodies,
we loved each other
beneath the city's first yawn, its warning,
its arrogant protest.
A tiny paper star
glowing on my lip.

V

You call me, love, and I grab a taxi,
cross February's dizzying
reality to see you.
The short-lived world offers
a seat in the back,
its sheltered vault of dreams,
lights flashing like conversations,
in the breeze signs switched on,
they're not where we're headed,
but they're written about us.

Now I know your words won't have
a generous tone, your hair's
restless feel
holds the false nostalgia
of the dim basement where you're waiting.
And, at last, tomorrow
when you wake up,
dreamy and with details
out of context,
you'll pity or fear yourself,
feel shame or dignity, hesitation
and perhaps lustful unease,
the blow left by
stories told one sleepless night.

Still we know it's worse,
riskier
to take them home, not hide their bodies
in bar smoke.

With no language I've come from my loneliness,
and with none I'll go toward yours.
There's nothing to say,

but I'm sure
we'll talk about it later,
undressed, playing it down,
kindling rhythms of the past,
the distant things
no longer to harm us.

XI

We're suspects. The first bus
went by, startled us
at the scene of the crime.
Unbound collars and hands
on the verge of dying give up.

The light stops us.
We feel its gun at our backs,
too indecisive,
its tremble in us, hidden
beneath the small forest of bedsheets.

Run!
Grab hold of love and run for your insides!
On your lips there's a lawless canyon,
a burning maze of exits.
Take a look at your heart or your waist,
that castle high up
crowned by my thighs like a lake of mist.

Run!
Heed only the currents of your skin
blowing by and then returning.
And let the storm sound,
let the shots sound,
let the sirens sound at your back.

XV

Your heart's closed for repairs
and goes wandering in the music.
It won't answer me.

A bandit from the start, it won't last
living beneath the metal
realm of words.

The glance it bore knew
the wandering ache
of night ships.

It turned into a witness when it told me
of the doubt in my eyes
and their hidden song.

It's silence, silence still,
void enchained
to the rays of the moon.

Which way will take me there
with no crossroads, no kilometers?
Where might I find it?

XX

The days take off their shoes
so they can walk past without us knowing.
They're practically good-byes, almost encounters
— nice but awkward ones —
of bodies watching each another
and postponing the date.
Still we tend to leave traces
that aren't memories behind.

From the untilled garden I keep
the man who came to desire you,
to walk without you,
wild and alone.
Because of you the oleander spoke to him,
with its branches, difficult like young girls,
and too the palm trees tall like your nakedness,
and the sky drawn closed
seeking
the light used by love to take in your eyes.

Let's never grow old. Maybe we won't.

And now he can tell you,
when you remind me of the oleander,
and your arched drawing recalls a palm,
and your eyes go cloudy
above the lovers' wild garden.

Maybe we won't grow old. Or maybe it's time
taking off its heels so to not cause trouble.
Or maybe it's desire
strolling over our lips still barefoot.

XXV

Remember you only exist in this book.

Thank my ghosts for your life,
the passion I put in each verse
when I remember the air you breath,
the clothes you put on and then take off me,
the taxis you hail each night,
the sirens and hearts of taxi drivers,
the drinks you share in bars
with the people who live on their countertops.
Remember I'm waiting on the far side
of the streetcars when you get in late,
the telephone, an awkward sentry,
becomes a guest with no news,
there's an empty noise of elevators
arguing alone, convening
while they raise or lower your nostalgia.
Remember my kingdom is all the doubts
in this city of swiftness alone,
and freedom, terrible swan,
isn't the night bird of dreams,
but complicity, its constant
saber wound making us
realize we're literary characters,
true lies, false truths.

Remember I exist because this book does.
I can kill us both by tearing out a page.

Second Book

XV

The lost kingdom
where any rule takes the shape of a kiss,
a private scar
behind the embraces,
governs us with its dreams,
from distance to distance.

I want you to rise
with the same impatience as trees,
up toward the perfect height
to brush against my lips, to search them
for the wet without the rain.

I know we'll discover
naked silhouettes around the house,
visiting reminders,
ghosts of a summerless night,
walking inside us, asking for explanations,

because darkness, like a mirror,
returns to us the image we give it.

Still I recognize all the questions
I don't know how to answer for you,
the body where interrogations live,
your dream in kerchiefs as if you've cried.

XVIII

Below the burnt out light,
your eyes are cold, you use them
to search for these October hours
and their garden stained with gin,
dry leaves, silences
speaking of us as they fall.

Because even if truth no longer exists,
though no one looks after the funeral,
there are nights when it does arrive,
an uncomfortable guest,
leaving us filthy, abandoned, out of cigarettes,
like a restaurant about to close,
chairs upturned.

"They're waiting for us."

I don't know how to answer you,
just that I'm aware of my own irony,
since a man is a wolf to himself too.

"They're waiting for us."

High above, silent, black vultures,
clouds waiting for us on the street.

XIX

Who's there?
Unfinished line in my verse,
neglected dream,
silence of lights and doors?

Who's there?
After parting, to endure
with battle eyes
below the dead shadow of keys?

Who's there?
Here unarrived, to desert
the tone of voice,
the unfinished sum of steps?

In those very lips who packed their bags
I sought the heroes of destiny.
They came one afternoon to take you with them,

and I understood nothing's understandable.

XXVI

In a cold, polygon rain,
with a sky high on storms
and outlying clouds.

Because this love of borrowed keys engulfs us
with a makeshift intimacy,
unfriendly walls,
objects like owls in the shadows.

They are
the saddest sheets on Earth.
Look
how people live.

XXVIII

You owe a letter to the south, like history.

I wonder about you, what you'd say
to me now, leaning against my shoulder,
considering the careless steps
of people in the park, their contours
when cold slips through
sickly tree trunks.

I miss your opinions nearby,
while kids shout, bundling up
with a school step, workers
inevitably walk faster,
ahead of maids, soldiers
mistake their clothes for
winter's sickly hues.

I'm not so sure now if you recall the racket
of distant stores, clean women
bent over with baskets,
or drink deliverers,
the poor street stalls
selling lies with
the sickly swiftness of habits.

And still it exists, you'd say,
the south exists in this park too,
taken by the cold, while all this passes by
like the necks of waiting youth:
the questions lifted,
the stubborn hopes,
the future's sickly secrets.

Invitation to Return

To go to hell there's no need
to change one's place or position.
                    RAFAEL ALBERTI

Whoever knows the winds, whoever fashions
a voice out of distance to hold memory,
whoever knows the skin of nakedness
like knowing the trace of a name,
and isn't frightened by it, and accompanies it
beyond the winter locked away in syllables,
suddenly like a kiss,
to rise through the mist by the bridge,
brush the fingers of a void,
head out to sea, lose
the fear of growing distant.

In the wave's weakened
violet dusk,
while old signs and lights
sink with the port,
our waiting conversations
will float in the water.
They'll be the forced disillusion
fallen from the spars with the wind,
return to memory
the storm of speaking
or words split like ship masts.

Since dreams leave remains
behind like shipwrecks,
with wood, bodies sunken in sheets,
filled with subject freedom.
It's not the foul city
pushing the sails. Not the heart either,
desire's primitive hut,

adventuring through lit-up islands
where the sea hides its ruins,
Baudelaire algae, foam and silence.
It's need, the lone
need of a man,
who brings us on deck,
makes us tremble, live in bodies
resisting the voices of Sirens,
tied to the bow,
with the helm groaning in our hands.

Leave, let's go far away,
with no illusion desperately calling,
without the pain taking on its decency.
Skin, my skin, the winds
have asked so much at the shore,
they've shattered so much in cities and chests,
they don't know countries, won't sing of them,
they don't recall nations,
only dreams.

I know their return
is undoubtedly ours. Because with a human voice,
like old sailors,
upon the blurry pain of their backs,
they'll come to tell us:
it's time,
let's return with the tide.

Twilight's courage and force
will carry you to the depths of what's already known,
and we'll see frigates over dark pools,
still the divided silhouette of a child
won't be fragile or fatigued.

So, after the journey,
surprised and quieted facing the ghost,
while old signs and lights
slowly turn up with the harbor,
we'll hear the song of those arriving,
of those who set foot where they've been
expected for so long.

And the sea, the sweet, tragic sea,
at the mercy of its own distance,
will know how to write
the journey was never our treasure,
or the famous pain in poems,
but dreams thrown to the street,
beds and their haze,
awakened from so many long nights
where only we could foretell,
speak of desires in shadow.

Near your hair, capital of winds,
history in two, din of tears,
all of it must be the necessary past,
distanced misery,
things to tell in a few years,
if someone actually asks about us.

Still, inevitably,
between the low night and this house
where I often write,
I'll wait for the lips
that call strangely to me once more to ask:

Prisoner of love, for whom do you carry
one shoulder of glass and another of oblivion?

From *The Flowers of Cold*

Crossed-Out Song

The man left when the moon
rested in the hands of the last minute.

There was cold,
silver pride crossing the street,
since the blinds
of consummate bars gave way.
As they folded, night abandoned in the porticos
echoes of old history with close characters.

Captive he walked down the street
of empty hours.
No longer in the company
of his shadow's leopard liquid
or steps heard.

Only the river bridge,
only the lowly garden at the riverbank,
only streets of polluted light,
shapeless, succeeding,
like water from a river.

The moon never knew how to explain
how the man escaped that early morning.

Bitter Song

On her face she wears
three years lost
and a six-o'clock-in-the-morning cold.

They're going to break your heart.
All at once
light switched off,
murky halls,
door sinking its noise into her back.

They're going to break her heart.
And she drags along
a dark chain
of frozen passions,
cold that only fits
behind a word.

I see her walking,
slowly
fading away into her affairs,
sadness on the run, coming and going
from the shadows to my front door.

On the street electric light leaves
the silent trembling
of three anchored ships.
When she passes by I hear
something like an oar's blow
and a murmur of water.

Song with No One

In 10-B
days don't break and nights
no longer dream of love or fear.

On the far side of dirty panes
no one knows about the missing woman.
Her walls give her up for disappeared.

A missing woman
and solitude's black swan
perching on a lake of unrented light.

No one will ever know.
Still someone passing by unaware
thinks the wind hangs with a stale scent.

Song of Mist

To Maite and Jesús

All at once it returns to her, the dream
of the man who was now someone else.

If he picks her up,
someone else gets out of the car.

The shadow on the stairs
climbs with someone else's steps.

The doorbell, the cold hand
and wedding band are someone else's.

When she opens the door for him,
the one who closes it is someone else.

She has nothing, only the dream
of the man who was now someone else.

Evicted Song

Yes,
you know evening falls
by the gazer's law of gravity.

And you know its light,
cheapened, cold,
like disheartened glass.

You hear it's seven o'clock.
From the world's metallic surface,
everything's aged.

The evening falls
like a kind of knowledge,

and it's an era too,
an overworked balance,
where life pushes more than the weight of dream.

And still the evening
falls yet more, sadly,
with the faint color of questions
with no answers,
which is the color of time,
the color of old buses
crossing the city.
They're like evenings
and drag their ambiguous paint behind them.

That's why your back's turned,
looking toward the void like all of us,
unfortunate, anonymous,
in the middle of the wait leading
your steps toward night:

and you no longer know
if night is

a difficult form of brilliance,
an evicted question,
or simply loneliness and cold.

Night Song

To Luis Antonio de Villena

December moon called-off
and suddenly rising,
pale above the night like a last
stage of consciousness:

you've seen knife's criminal
cold flash
and know in me a junkie's
busy blood.
No giving needless verse
to solitude,
but instead wallpaper and a void
of sordid apartments
no longer in search of will or dream.
Moon called-off,
tasting of farewell,
confirm the strange
freedom her slumbering cheek
leaves on my chest.
Add melancholy to our embrace
so there's something
too of fullness when memory
returns to me this night
of unexpected daze.

Certify it now.
Stamp the invoice of shadows
and rooms,
while my heart vanishes
like my home,
before you return to the enigma
on the far side of clouds
and I feel once more the careful
slowness of being alone,
hateless, loveless, called-off.

Verlaine Song

This rain has no heart
or night to fall on.

You see it walking around penniless,
like a stranger's solitary shadow,
with windows in profile, treading
the sand of it own remoteness.

It has no heart to fall on.
Only blind words
that dissolve names, useless
for telling its journey's futile founding.

The rain has no tale, doesn't understand
it comes from the past. I see it
walking stone silence,
slipping past in search
of the echo of a warehoused light
in any open bar.

It asks no one. It doesn't dare.
Lost in the enigma of its steps,
it seems like a stranger.
No love or hostility. And yet
this falling rain
has the sensation of being
here before,
of knowing
hours unreal,
cities with no heart
or night to fall on.

Furniture Store

To Silvia and Felipe

In the furniture store
are a thousand empty houses. Mirrors,
the polished perfection of tables
and dressers,
Dali's Christ, watercolors,
armoires, beds, everything sleeps
with the restless nostalgia of its square meters.
Clock chimes leaping
with no one to call,
would also like
to live on schedule, a domestic
version of time tomorrow.

It's May in the gardens. A couple
keeps watch over their lips with a pearly glance,
forages among the doubts leading
to the first kiss,
the one they've pondered at night
and repeated, natural, burning,
like an unconscious gesture.

Later there are months, picture-perfect,
dressed-up, running to a date.
In August distance sparks
love letters. But September,
accomplice of trees, offers
a knowledge of plazas and gardens,
and autumn light
is like a thwarted embrace,
trembling, confused,
like the hours at Alberto's house.
No one's there tomorrow.
You already know who he is,
my best friend from work.

To see you naked
or fathom the hollow of your hands.
I'm not scared because I love you.
I like you with the lights on.
It's still early,
call me when you get there.
I'm going to hang up, my mother
needs the phone.

Meddlesome Saturday moon
leans on the 127's glove box
and falls slowly
over our shoulders
like serenaded lights over a disco.
Yet winter sun is beautiful
too on Sunday mornings.
My parents want to meet you,
we've been together for two years.
I can get a job, maybe we'll get by
with my salary and your rosy lips.
Yesterday I found a place,
sweetheart, to see you naked
is to fathom the hollow of my hands,
balconies facing a river, little by little
we'll furnish it. I'd like to.
How many monthly payments,
to grow old with you in this house,
in this room, in this kiss.

In the furniture store
are a thousand empty kisses. Help me choose.
Look at the big bed, held close,
the sofa of infinite evenings,
an armoire that can
fold seasons and put them away.

How much will it all cost?
The family table, look at the mirror
to measure the kids.
We can sign the papers,
sweetheart, it's your nakedness
dividing this map of bedsheets.
To follow, age, dream life
in the percentage of an embrace.

The house's furniture
will be happiness, vivid memory,
until the hidden dream of a child arrives,
the one that founds time
and returns at night,
natural, burning with primitive prints,
eternal values
bought on installment
and maybe a little marked down.

Loose Adaptation of Immortality

Deep in the night,
like a sleepy caress surprises
and becomes something more,
shadows with the heat of matter
biting their lips, hastily removed
pajamas and a wild darkness
burning between arms.

In half light, outlines
like the love of a generous dream
with its characters,
slowly sketched,
while thought moves quicker
than bodies, making clear
where the next caress will be,
when and how and with what words might there be peace.

In open, full light,
distanced from me to watch us,
watch you sunken, locked away
with your own senses,
until you open your eyes
overflowing with lonesome clarity,
and like me the room's observant,
and in your eyes you understand
we want to watch you like a river,
a pale evening,
an infinite landscape.

Neither of us believes
in immortality. Still there are moments
—dark ones, of penumbra or full light—
when we brush up against the world of books,
the rewards of eternity.
I write this poem to celebrate

past and present
still overlapping with us,
living recollections
and kisses as golden as the ones
from our memory.

Nocturne

With something of savage insolence
silence surprises me,
a domestic Friday darkness
suddenly interrupted.

I turn off the light.
For a moment
I lean against the wall, and settled in
over the slow night
I close my eyes like closing a book.
At my back I know
the heat of objects undone,
behind the curtain
shines the useless shadow rising from the street.

At this very door
I've often felt sorrow. I know the sinister,
tormented peace
of the lonely chair,
its untimely betrayals of friendship,
and the rest of the story
lingers to burn again and again
cluttered on the table.
And though my steps are unsettled too,
today's hall
doesn't seem a tunnel: it's dark
like imprecise words,
like August nights with jasmine.

In remembrance
of its amazing scent of survival,
I want to walk through the house
and undress in the dark
so I won't disturb anything,
not even turn on the mirror lights,

so I won't wonder
what's the use of an oasis,
if my heart knows the desert
awaiting it
like ancient traces now before us.

Welcome
warmth under the covers,
known presence in half-sleep,
body of some sufficient days!
Today your outline
settling in next to mine and desirable sleep
is enough, while I cloudily
think of the drunken moon
and the man who finds
the cold scent of tobacco upon his waking.

From *Separate Rooms*

The Traveler's Reasons

He's alone. To be on his way
he's detached from things.
He carries no provisions.

When day's passed,
at evening's end he thinks of all that's happened.
He's only stirred
by the unexpected triumph
of living his own life
in the certain fate of his consciousness,
naturally, free of debts or flags.

Once he said love.
His lips swelled with ash.

He said tomorrow too
with eyes denying the present
and he only had shadows to clasp,
ghosts as balance,
a pathway of clouds.

Loneliness, freedom,
two words that often lean on
the traveler's wounded shoulders.

He takes everything in hand, is swayed by nothing.
Today his traces bear the burn
of empty dreams.

He won't give up. To go on his way
he admits life takes shelter
in a room that's not his.
Light always lingers behind a window.
Through the door
he often hears night's footsteps.

He knows he needs
to learn to live in another age,
in another love,
in another time.

A time of separate rooms.

The Mirrors

To Luis Muñoz

No matter if you've gotten a good night's sleep or not
hotel mirrors never forgive,
they're like wild animals,
they refuse human contact.

Even so, the glow of family mirrors
takes pity on us,
helps us to fake it, forgives us
out of affection or habit.

I know mirrors are the stagnant
water of a flowing river.
I've seen how the reverberating sun
can hide the sludge of shadows.

Still, whoever looks into the depths of our eyes
sees time's crevices, the spiders
of a past all at once arising
in hotel mornings to offend us.

Why answer? Close your eyes.
There's nothing that makes you age
more than your own glance.

First Day of Vacation

I was swimming in the sea and it was late,
just at that moment
when lights float like embers
of a worn-out fire
and questions, strange silences
burn in the water.

I'd decided to swim to the red
buoy, hidden like the sun
on the other side of ships.

Far from the beach,
solitary and lost in twilight,
I went deep into the ocean
feeling the unease that moves
me when I'm deep into a poem
or a long night of unknown love.

And suddenly I saw her over the waters.
An older woman
with a tired beauty
and white hair pulled back,
she drew nearer swimming
with serene strokes.
She seemed to come from the horizon.

As she passed me,
she stopped a moment and looked into my eyes:
I haven't come for you,
it's not you yet.

The market's clamor and the roar of a motorcycle
desperately crossing the street awoke me.
It was mid-morning,
the sky was clear and seemed

a living flag
on August's mast.
I went down to breakfast at the terrace
on the waterfront
and considered the racket of people,
the sea like a raft,
bodies below the sun.
In the paper,
the name of the drowned man wasn't mine.

The World So Often

Nothing glows in the day's shadows
like someone's story,
nothing tends to explain
the world so often.

Her father's in Paris,
her mother (they're separated) has lived for years
in South Dakota,
where she went to look for her at eighteen,
when French law allowed.

She has an apartment she rents
for four hundred dollars a month,
an old car,
a tiny scar,
solitude on her lips
and she came to New Mexico to study Spanish.

In the hotel windows
little by little night's gleaming
turned to objects.
A strip mall landscape
came into view, murmur after murmur,
slowly, just
as if reality had confessed.
Freeways and trailer homes,
a difficult landscape
for any of us.

Chance,
who knows no homeland, took
the liberty of introducing us
one rainy afternoon in Albuquerque.
She told the story of her life
like someone growing a tree at the edge of a road.

I keep the promise I made her
and write this poem.

The Insomnia of Jovellanos

Bellver Castle, April 1, 1808

Since I know dreams rot,
I've left dreams behind.
The sea still shifts on the shore.

Seasons pass like aimless traces,
useless winter light,
useless summers.
My shadow goes by too, following itself
through the solitary castle,
like the black print left on walls
by years and wind.
Seasons, my life's memories,
the sea comes and erases us.

The sea still shifts in the night,
when it's only repeated murmur,
a distant hunch locked away in eyes
and hiding in the silence of my cell
all things combined,
cowardliness, dream, nostalgia,
what returns to the shore after shipwrecks.

On the edge of light, when it dawns,
I search in the sea
and the sea is a sword
and from my eyes launch
the ships that have been born from my nights.
Some go toward Spain,
kingdom of pyres and superstitions,
futureless past,
still aching in the hands of the present.

Winter is the time of meditation.

Other ships sail the coasts of France,

there where dreams rot
like a trampled flower,
where freedom
was the rose of all the gallows
and the most beautiful fruit left a bitter taste.

Summer is the time of meditation.

The sea still shifts. I search for
my time among two waves,
the flexible world of the shore,
withholding its steps for a moment,
nothing more than a moment,
between reality and its edges.

I know,
sad meditations of a captive . . .
I wouldn't know how to deny it.
Imprisoned and ill, defeated,
I cry for the want of my homeland,
my few friends,
everything my heart loved.

On the very horizon
where days surface and light
caresses pines and warms my cell,
night and its shipwrecks surface too.
My days and nights are the time
of meditation.

Since I know dreams rot
I've left dreams behind,
still I close my eyes and the sea keeps shifting
and with it my desire
and I can imagine

my freedom, the coasts of the Cantabrian,
the steps growing distant on the beach
or the conversation between two friends.

There,
barely touched by the water,
I'll write my traces in the sand.
They won't last long, I know,
nothing more than a moment.

The sea will shroud us,
yet the traces will be of one happier
in a freer land.

From *Completely Friday*

Monday Man with a Secret

This calm, quick April Monday,
early morning, sleepless.
The work hour vulture
walks by the café.
Among coffee cups, toast and newspapers
they talk about the latest news,
and the man with a secret
plunges into the new week's tunnel.
He strips wellbeing from his coffee,
smiles at whomever looks at him, finds comfort
in having a secret.

Young bodies are the present,
still the chance innocence of their conversations
comes to us versed in the past.
On his way to work
the man with a secret gets it,
when students fill the bus
and a turmoil of clean-faced bodies
takes over Monday.
He watches them grow, studies
a restlessness soon fading
from time's profit,
like a spark of the unknown in their eyes.
To live is to fold flags.

The man with burning eyes
is wounded by academic roses,
in between greetings, daggers and cypresses
he crosses campus,
walks the halls searching for his room,
teaches his class.
But he's got a secret
and the 19th century becomes
a matter of fear,

poems breaking loose from the page,
lines appearing at the top
of a mid-air glance,
someone who's left notes
and textbooks behind,
to clench his fists until he's wounded
by another crueler
living rose,
the rose of a secret in the soul of a Monday.

He opens his office door
and his books smile like old accomplices.
He's read in them what he feels,
just maladjusted literature.
But not this time,
because not tonight,
not this morning.
The man with a secret looks in the mirror
when he gets up,
discovers the enigma of his strange, burning eyes
and says no,
not this time.

The city? Open
with light, body flung,
has changed its skin in the window.
It's no longer patience, nighttime alley,
or skeptical traffic's work day.
So he goes to the phone,
searches for the blue ink of the number written
on his driver's license,
the condition of a Monday
that no longer cares about dates,
but fruit, taste on lips.

The man with a secret dials and says:
"Hi. Good morning. It's me. I'm done."

Confessions

I waited for you.
Beyond the winter of fifty-eight,
the rhythmless lyrics and the summer
of my first letter,
through slow halls and exams,
books, afternoons with soccer,
flower refusing to become pillow,
beyond the boy bound to the moon,
beneath everything I loved,
I waited for you.

I'm waiting for you.
On the far side of nights and streets,
trampled leaves,
public works
and people's remarks,
beyond everything I am,
a few restaurants we don't go to anymore,
more rushed than the time that escapes me,
closer to light and earth,
I'm waiting for you.

I'll be waiting.
Like autumn yellows,
still a word of love before the silence,
when skin's snuffed out,
when love embraces death
and our pictures turn more serious,
above memory's slope,
after my mind becomes sand,
behind the last lie,
I'll be waiting.

August's City

Finally the plane starts to descend,
I'm going to August's city.
The shadows of wings leave blue traces
over the dry earth
and course above fields with the shakiness
of an old movie.
I'm going
to the city taken by bare arms.
I'm going to the slowness of museums,
to terraces that plant a flash of beer
in the trees.
I'm in the city of heat you put up with,
in the city that lives to the rhythm of transfers.
Santa Isabel Street, number 19,
where taxis gather with their hunting
dog look
and the stairs have the will
of a clenched fist,
a fist clenched because maybe
it's hiding a jewel,
a memory-colored emerald,
a dream to defend,
like two bodies defend
when they embrace,
like two bodies love
with a storm's painstaking will,
like two bodies that already know
the time they'll never forget,
the metal caribbean of fans,
the shadow of their blades on the ceiling,
or the blue traces,
the wings of a plane taking off again,
in August's city,
on the second floor,
in a corner of the wind.

Doubtful Urban Geography

It doesn't look like scenery
but the broken down, arid
description of scenery.

With dirty walls.
With the cruelty of a taxidermist sun
at three in the afternoon.

Intercoms,
old balconies, department store names,
a closed bar.

August wields
its realistic lantern and distance,
just like someone walking by.

Madrid, empty street,
tale of displays and billboards,
hidden clocks.

Because there's a corner
where memory and imagination
like to meet,

and footprints sink
until they trample, I don't know, hesitantly,
the awareness of time.

Winter fits
in a shop window, autumns flow,
spring moves

summer's wheels.
It's a feeling, only a moment,
still there are shadows and days

to leave the movie theater,
to grow in an old porch,
to get bored
or be happy and see you
coming home from school
one rainy evening.

It's your city. All of a sudden
I'm walking until I get lost on the streets
of someone else's memory.

A shadow in my shadow,
your time goes by again and becomes mine.
Sometimes it happens

after a poem too.
Words become streets
in the shadow of time.

That time speaks our language,
but pronounces our names
with a foreign accent.

Tuesday and Literature

An empty chair at a talk
has eyes and gazes out with absolute coldness.
Especially if you're on the other side
of the blue on the map,
separated from me by nighttime cities,
fields of clouds, ship lights,
shorelines drawn with foam
and homes with swimming pools.

A plane flies over
dawn's muddy red
just like dream flies over your night,
near and so far,
searching for another land not mine,
even though it's near me.
Sometimes I wonder if I'm the one
pretending to be me when I live in your dreams.

The water's poured. My presenter's excesses
leave me facing the audience.
It's a Tuesday in October. I'm supposed to talk
about the usefulness of poets
and in the empty chair
doesn't sit Becquer's silence bound in an album,
or the defenseless multitude
stuck in a bottle by Baudelaire,
like a ship,
like smoke,
dawn's muddy red.

What sits in the chair is your memory,
along with the imagination of the north wind
chasing after you now, the streets watching you,
and the closets
where you find your reflection.

I'm where you are, but in life
some things you can't share.
That's why I'm still here and with you,
near and so far,
searching for another world not mine,
even though it's near me.

Poetry is the voice of those who know
they're alive and mortal, Blas de Otero said so,
and in conclusion, Gentlemen, a poem
isn't born from the struggle to speak alone,
it's the need to speak
to an empty chair.

Saturday Night Crime

On the broken mirror
a bloody footprint.
Light showed up
and didn't recognize me
because I had night
inside. I was
the shadow of a shadow.
I was frightened
of what could happen
next to a shadow.

I've broken so many things in my life.

When I was frightened
I saw the house.
I already said I saw blood,
chairs overturned,
drawers opened,
books piled up,
bottles, dried flowers,
shattered glass on the floor.
Like a tiger the night that I was
leapt at me.

I've broken so many things in my life.

Fear never fails.
Like a pro,
it knew where to sign me up
and called my name.
Snake skin
slipped through my fingers.
Where was your body?
In what kind of a hostile place
did the night that was me

hide my crime?

You looked like you'd drowned,
definitive, noble,
like hair
hovering with the moon.
But you got up,
gave me your hand,
and we walked through the house.
I got to the place in my dream
that's most yours,
and lied still beside you.

I've broken so many things in my life.

Impossible Song

Since memories have shadows,
the shadows of mine warned me
when I thought of leaving the reef.
I walked barefoot over the fire
of an impossible story.

A friend mentioned it
with his good sense of dead truths,
cynical and sad
from the rain sullying the glass
of the impossible story.

The enemy said
to anyone who listened to his sermons,
convictions like fists.
He let the wolves run through the fields
of futureless love.

And both our cities
proved it too, confused
by the senseless past
of brothels and secret nights.
A futureless love.

Now I know how to answer you:
plenitude bears two edges,
to kill or commit suicide.
This world's miserable enough
without the risk of eternally being
the impossible story of a futureless love.

The City

They're made of concrete and glass,
strange places and busy people.
In each a tree grows
in front of a suicide's house
and there're kids used to falling asleep
dreaming of a dog.
There're always breakfasts in luxury hotels,
families with front yards,
but even more common
are dark porches with couples,
cold kisses,
concrete rose in the window.

Streets lead to decaying plazas,
Sunday afternoons in cafés
and car exhaust in the eyes of a madman
murmuring his years,
endlessly counting them
from one subway station to the next.
Coming out of the tunnels we think
the rainy skies
are like a letter from the past,
and we understand
life is a slow, double-edged sword
in the footsteps of no one,
empty nights
or the weakness cities have
for neighborhood movie theaters
and heavily made-up ticket clerks.

Despite the plane trees, the elms, the lindens,
despite the lawns, if we're talking about the North,
the people watching us,
the people running red lights,
flowing by storefronts,

need the shelter
of another kind of vegetation,
a reserve of numbers and credit cards
spreading their roots in basements
and seeking solitude in lofts
like furniture and ancient rats.

Traveling isn't pointless.
It's true every city
wakes up in a similar way,
but night comes
differently.
During the day you can see
secretaries, janitors, police officers,
street musicians and soldiers,
salesgirls listening and smiling,
office clerks with their scent of petitions,
drivers, strange priests,
disgraced executives.
Just like anywhere
because kilometers barely exist.
Still night exists too,
solitude wipes out professions
in a world populated only by
men and women,
secrecies of bitter courage.

In the city you can find
clocks that stop at the last drink,
the moon over a taxi
and every poem I write to you.

The Car

I don't know what's going on
in the red car that's climbed the hill
and stopped beneath the chestnut trees.
I don't know what's going on
but the dogs stopped barking
and the evening got longer:
first a city,
its paintwork of towers and domes
in a streak of countryside,
then light's violet gentleness,
later on the infinite.

Like time on watch hands,
the car rolls by and gets lost in the world's arms.
Maybe it's shared river's mystery,
flowing memory,
distance of water and hours.
Our first summer
was a time of secrets and roads.
In matters of love
you need a secret to tell it all.
We disappeared inside ourselves,
didn't leave the sun, or the freeways,
or the dry landscape of our backs.
With my second car
I understood my luck
of not belonging, for a few hours,
to oaks or poplars,
bridges or changes of meaning,
the unending line,
the reflection
of speed in car windows.
Only words
on a trip to our past incognito,
the luck of having belonged

to the world, and then
to not answer,
only words in a car,
no buildings or olive trees, only
the way of telling each other everything
we haven't shared,
the years we missed,
names of towns, people
changed to memory,
addresses and book titles.
Only words with their frequency,
modulating time, crossing one other,
trying to tune in
when they come and go
as the kilometers pass by
like radio stations.

And maybe the mannequins and farmers,
the crowds of traffic lights,
and the kids on the bridge
watched us
not knowing our love
went by in shifting history,
words surrounded by arms,
the intimacy of vertigo,
our last refuge.

Words are caves in speed,
they hold secret water,
especially if they spring from the past,
like that red car
climbing the hill
and stopping beneath the chestnut trees.
I don't know what's going on
but the dogs stopped barking

and the evening got longer
behind the windshield:
first the city,
its paintwork of towers and domes
in a streak of countryside,
then light's violet gentleness,
later on the infinite.

Immortality

I've never had gods,
never felt the cruel
will of heroes.
For so long
my judge's chair was free.
I never expected a trial
where I'd have to account for my days.

Determined to live, I sought the shadow
skilled at taking me in
during summer and the fire willing
to sweep winter away with it.
I spent silent, vigilant nights
unhurried,
I let the circle of years go by.
I was convinced
existing had no transcendence,
since light's always on the run
more than darkness,
a brilliance in the midst of the void.

Suddenly trees with insistent glances
lit up in the forest,
the sea grew lips of sand
just like words whispered in a corner,
the wind opened its hands
and the hotels their rooms.
The earth seemed barer,
because night was,
like the void,
a dark brilliance in the midst of light.

Then I understood immortality
could charge you up front.
An immortality not residing

in statue-filled plazas,
religious clouds
or plasticized literary vainness,
bursting with homicidal praise
and cocktail murmurs.
My reasons are different. I don't want a reader
who's never seen the earth moved to tears
in the midst of an embrace.

The glass
you placed face down on the table
holds a time of hindered gold.
Life's enough to justify me.
When I'm called to testify,
even if it's only an empty chair listening,
my voice will stay strong.

Not for what death promises,
but for all it can't take away from me.

The Night

Now we feel it to be inexhaustible
like an ancient wine
and no one can contemplate it without vertigo
and time has charged it with eternity.
Jorge Luis Borges

With their plotting,
with dreams never remembered
and those that are,
with the insomnia of drainpipes,
with a trembling worry the second after
a wolf's howl
or the frightened warning of dogs,
with shadow crossing the empty yard,
with the wicked moon, with love, men
raised the night.

With skyscraper windows,
with a monk's prayer,
with the weary clothes of a whore,
with a jazz orchestra in the basement
of the sleeping city,
with a shutter in the storm,
with Borges's verses
and a drunk's confessions,
with the June moon, with hate,
they raised the night.

And with the North Star far above ships too,
with the philosopher's ruminations,
with tribes sitting round a fire,
with the perversity of an informer,
and with time imprisoned
in the first embrace, in the first tears,
in the first names of an interrogation,

with the yellow light,
with the silence of hospitals,
they raised the night.

With your nakedness too. The distinct
perfection of the night in your nakedness
proves to me destiny's frail conviction,
since the universe's aim
was to call us here.
Every single night exists in one white night.
Inescapable time has passed
to abandon your slumber in this bed,
so I can see in your eyes the blaze
of an endless night.

The Past

After passing by
the last humbled houses
and suffering the mist
of clear-cuts and garbage dumps,
the road climbs toward cleaner air
favoring the moon that's been held up
now for quite some time.
When the headlights turn
toward trembling olive groves,
images of war still switch on,
machine guns in their rat's nests,
nighttime trucks,
and further up,
above days and dates,
a murmur of words,
a time of poets and republic,
of civil will on chalkboards
and dignity, a melancholy
suddenly forsaken,
near Víznar,
in this ravine's mass grave.

We reach our ancestors
through carnivorous seas of dried lemons
and in them history is
a river of geography.
There are those who seek out cities,
the ballad of forests and green mountains,
a house's empty closet,
flag or anthem.
I come back to this moon hanging
over olive groves and your car.

This is where my dead live,
these are my roots

and their heat spreads
like branches at the edge of the road,
rain-rusted wires
I still use to hang out my clothes.
Look, let me show you
the echo of your skin when I kiss you.
The city's in flames, it bears the coldness
of cowardly years.
A girl folds
a soldier's defeated uniform.
She doesn't know whether to hide or keep it.
Maybe one day she'll find,
in the box of dried lemons,
one more chance.

Poetry

Poetry's useless, it's only good
for cutting off a king's head
or charming a young girl.

Maybe it's good
for streaking water with dream,
that is if water's death.
And if time grants it the only material it's got,
it just might be a good knife,
because a clean cut's better
when we slash memory's skin.
With a piece of broken glass
desire
makes for dirtier wounds.

You're poetry,
a clean cut,
a streak in the water
—that is if water really is a reason to exist—,

the woman who lets herself be charmed
into cutting off a king's head.

Politics

I've never had a beard. Not even in that picture
you're so amusedly gazing at now.
The boy with
brash, bothered eyes,
a turtleneck,
long hair
and a doubtful cigarette, maybe a joint.

Just starting college,
all of us were smoke.
Smoke of clandestine classrooms,
smoke of celebrated books,
smoke of nights and bonfires
where we burned
prayer books, fears,
post-war customs,
winters and politicians
who over the years had
soured their lack of color
on television.

Everything was smoke
and a beard grew just like optimism.
When the yard rots
and a poison dirtier than November
injects its yellow
into the silence of reality,
cities fall asleep thinking of the future.
That's how strange paradises crop up.

Like it was today,
like we were all still arguing
behind closed doors,
I remember everyone had a turn,
commanding voices and revolution,

horizon of palm trees
on a poster of Juan's
plastered all over the street.
Naivety no doubt,
the smoke of impatient beings,
but also memories of skin,
life under way,
tattered kisses on Angel Street
at a time of big decisions.
We refused to cut our youth,
to place it
like a flower
in a nice vase.
Sometimes you can go along with
with the sea and forests.

I've never had a beard.
I've never born heaven's light,
but it's where I come from, like you,
more out of contempt than faith,
weary of power degrading us
and those in power smiling,
the likeable knife
and love in lofts,
fear's wicked lessons,
hairspray on heads,
cold glances
and solitude in cities
that fall asleep from gray and ash
in search of a strange heaven.

The same history
to kiss the flags and later carry them off,
brought me your body.

I'm still at the front door
more out of contempt than faith,
but now the emptiness left by flags,
living in absolute doubt,
none of it bothers me.
Down through the people's history,
the bar counter,
or television screens,
I descend toward the world with you.
Neither of us pledges
to argue the opposite,
yet a dreamer's realism
damned us to doubt
law-abiding citizens,
the hungry hearts of the sentimental,
exploiters in color
and a cynic's intelligence.

Sometimes you can go along
with forest clearings,
especially in the eyes of a boy
full of brashness,
with a turtleneck,
long hair
and a doubtful future
in his photos.

Old Age

At the cabin in the Sierra Nevada,
when I turned fifteen
my grandfather gave me his dagger,
the wolf's head
with worn-out silver plating.
He marked my height
on the north wall,
the one facing the lake.

One seventy five
and my eyes saw life ahead,
a heart with no moss,
growing up.

I remember his words of melting snow.
With the evening sun
during restless years,
the thirsty reflection of that silver wolf
went down to the shore.
My grandfather
who now held life in his hands,
fragile like a fishing pole,
spoke of returning,
paired old age with youth,
locked the future in his memory.
Time is a mountain path
winding up toward the top,
to let us fall down the other side.

When moss mistakes a heart
for the back wall of a house,
when eyes hold a liquid glance,
the roads turn back and once more we are
as tall as when we were fifteen.

That's why I stopped
at the logger bar
the first day we went
together to the cabin
and bought this dagger,
another wolf's head,
to offer you
the old wound on the back wall,
edges of time and age,
a pact with light,
more devoted than blood.

I'll go with you
down toward the reflection of me at fifteen.
It'll make sense
growing small over the cold water
of memories and its shapes.
At the thirsty side of light
you can find a hint of heat,
shelter in the snow,
if mouths descend at once
going out painlessly
to the rhythm of a history and its beginnings.

It's unbelievable the lake skin
bears no mark of a reflection.
Bodies won't forget it all,
time shared in dignity,
October storms
and spring thaws,
in a common world, long and spoken.
They won't forget
the secret man and woman,
their hotels lived in nighttime countries,
the private landscapes

of an invaded home,
the public shadows,
light's shipwreck,
open luggage.

A yellow apple, blacklisted,
keeps its red age,
shiver of the first time
in the last kiss.

It'll surely be
like standing at the foot of the lake,
faces joined,
on one of those endless evenings
where stars are born,
while the friendly night
arrives in the shape of a voice
drawing closer
to tell us:
come on,
let's get out of here.

From *Inner Life of the Snake*

On Turning Forty

So fierce, so untimely,
your twenty years break free from the photo
and demand explanations.
You hold the glance of my shadows
in eyes wounded by brilliance,
with the insolence of your prophecies
you scorn my memory's faithfulness,
through glassy skin
you flood the weariness of mine
and define my years by betrayals.

Stop making a scene,
we'll talk if you want.
Choose the weapons, the setting
for the conversation,
wait for the guests
to go to the cold dinner
of my forty years.
Evaporating,
like the dirty water of puddles
is drawn up to clouds,
I'll walk with you
to the plaza of your youth.
There, the glorious
trees of science and letters
with their words in the month of May,
and the order of numbers
at the shores of time,
closer to addition than division.

I imagine your voice, envision the air
—sometimes it returns to my lips
on overgrown nights—
you use to claim
all freedom is stone,

no need for wind or reasons
but willingness at the helm,
to cry out later on that my consciousness
is just wash on the line,
words hung out to dry.

You're right. I don't even say
half of what I feel.
But remember my loneliness,
ablaze in the lamp of the missing,
is the silence of public causes.
You can understand me:
my sleeping women,
drawer of defenseless ships,
an old telephone . . .
Every crossing-out looks
like the worry you suffer
before a blank life.

Since your light breaks open my shadows,
understand my silence in your cries.
Because you know I know
the delicate side of boldness,
what imitation there is in your faith,
the certainty that comes from others
pushing you
with the urgency to be chosen,
the desire to be liked,
even to live by hearsay.

I'll accept your complaints if you admit
the legitimacy of the slander.

Now that I must
ponder what I believe

in search of a sufferable fate,
I draw nearer to you,
you knew how to ponder your doubts.
When you get to the age soon to come,
you'll admit there's a time for fitting in,
worn, resistant skin,
the low tones of a voice,
and a heart, tired of choosing
from standing shadows or kneeling light.

After what I've seen and what you will,
it's not a bad outcome, I promise.
Come down to the day with me,
come to the real setting
where we'll talk,
and you'll thank me
for the difficult task of your survival.

Corner 40 Song

On corner 40,
between Minnesota Department Store
and the wine shop,
the night wind
of a sleepless light blows through.

Yesterday the García family
painted the walls of the first floor.
On the third,
two Germans from West Berlin
and a mumble of plastic.
On the second, the wind
of a sleepless light blows through.

No one remembers it now.
Letters from Barcelona and Bilbao
holding Bolivian necklaces,
trains headed North
are ships arriving from Morocco.
History refused to remember the past,
it's not fair to the fair-minded
or the freshwater river,
and it leaves with the wind of a sleepless light.

On the corner of wind,
in the eyeless city
where the windows
of a hamburger joint and a tavern meet,
solitude blows through
along with the night fire of a sleepless light.

Sun Song

Garbage dump sun, lowly animal
licking mountains
of wounded papers and withered words
with the meekness of an empty bottle,

you are the master of dawn.

Old sun disgraced
among beams of twilight
so the law of rot, so memory and mud
spin round you,

you are the master of dawn.

Sidetrack sun,
so harsh toward ruins with a childhood
like a cardboard horse motionless
beneath the tools in search of rust,

you are the master of dawn.

Through the chaos of your waters
sails the dark swan
blind to melancholy.

Waiting Song

I watch out for the song
wary to come.
I've sat down to bide my time almadraba fishing.

Patience is a blue-blooded lady.
She sits with me on this sooty, gray
rock almadraba fishing.

I've sat down to wait
for the tide and stealthy moon
that dreams while almadraba fishing.

I don't share silence.
I don't know what to say.
I've sat down to bide my time almadraba fishing.

2001 Song

Newspapers are
long winter nights.

My words burn in the brilliance.

On TV
when it rains it pours,
precisely where earth
doesn't know rain.

The coldness of the sermon
has uncovered roses, punishments, miracles
in the tainted rules of objectivity,
and now it sells news
instead of white sand in castaway's footsteps
or freedom in cemeteries.

They're the rules
and the sea won't forget them.
I await you in the light of an imperfect past.
You arrive in the shadows of a lost future.

Pornographic Song

To Benjamín

Water seeks edges to prop up its brow,
night searches out dreams to enter houses,
light becomes murmur
and countries play cards.

They play
like silence does with its sounds
to think they exist in a definite order.
Like moon rays
since they sing their number and come undone.

They play like gods unpunished,
beg for the color of a flag
and the shadow of an anthem.

In need of sovereignty
the naked aren't silver paper.
Shadows no longer lurk behind embraces
and countries play cards.

New Year's Eve (1940, 1970, 2000)

To Joaquín,
suppose I'm talking about us.

The serpent that did sting thy father's life
Now wears his crown.
                SHAKESPEARE

The city suspected itself.

Turning its head,
the winter from back then
surprised its own fleeing on the street,
the eyes of bridges watched over the river,
tables over tables,
the past over the past,
and words
measured their words
by the illnesses of rooms,
like mothers fearing tuberculosis.

Who are we?, asked the snow,
until it went blank
and proved roofs were
horizonless interrogations,
anxieties of keys
that have lost their doors.

The room of the shamed
belongs to the orders of smoke.
They don't live in peace or defeat,
perhaps between the wings of an insect
burnt by light,
when it learned, urged on by death,
truth is an empty place
trampled by fear and victors.

The sea was there too, but refused
to abandon the liquor bottles.
When the winter night
spread the tablecloth and arranged the chairs,
feigning its intention
to receive the year
just like the one left behind,
songs fell
like a secret legacy,
for not only did those who were
there embrace,
stuck in the skin of every house.

Those who were there weren't alone.

A star came down too,
wounded by the tips of deleted names,
and stayed silent,
listening to the sounds of the rooms.
Someone's coming up. Perhaps a threat
or maybe a brother returning from the shadows.

It was nineteen forty,
and it came like usual, with twelve tolls of the bell,
even though a wind of hunger and flags
had asked it
for papers.

In that universe of lead soldiers,
the world went round
the Puerta del Sol
—slow like a rusty song—
while in clocks
rains of an inevitable April
erased the snow of empty hours,

strange black snow where silence curdled.

Another air
began to file away at light's nails.

And it so happens that December's smoke
not only marked Spain's destiny
but my own history too,
the murmur of past and present
running like water over my eyes,
wash water,
water from rivers and washers,
water carrying out
the substitutions of memory
first called victory
and later on life.

There are cleaner tablecloths on the table,
and in the street cars
coming from Germany or Barcelona,
and on lips words
hanging from another light and music,
like Christmas decorations,
to light up the circle of days,
what is felt and said
with the sea in a glass
to celebrate the swell
and new years.

Ashes lived
like tired wolves on TV.
There were anthems,
saints and the Caudillo,
behind his imperial world of swords and mist,
ill, held

in the fragility of useless wood.
For a moment broken, it seemed
like they were left countryless.

Since freedom
was a way of knowledge
and love a day with no ring
from horizons to lips.
Almost a tragic story
with a happy ending.

That dream lived
as long as nights last, startled
among poverty's pride
and the cautious heart of luxury.

We went out to the balcony. The twelve tolls,
foam cleared of broken glass,
fallen on the plazas of the seventies.

What began to break?
More than the dirty mirrors of police stations
and waiting rooms,
where the dictatorship's poor people
dressed up in their Sunday suits.
Much more than silence,
the crucifix in the bedroom,
the pictures of a big family
and the order of which kids
should go to college first.

Much more . . . I've come to find out
contemplating the light of daybreak
in the eyes of a swan
with the look of a hyena.

The serpent that stung my father's life
now wears his crown.
Not the snake from the garden with
the tree of life and knowledge,
but the one hiding in the undergrowth
of happiness and numbers,
to infect time
until it's paralyzed.

Only reality
needs the deprived law of imagination
in its days and nights.
That's why anyone who tries to quell
our imagination
ought to deprive us of reality.
We're left without lies,
existing, more beautiful and blond,
in a world of pure inexistence.

Seagulls at riverbanks,
happy with the freshwater,
don't ask about the new year.

Since snow
is never innocent,
and nothingness isn't either,
dirty nothingness
blanketing gardens and table linens,
though it doesn't thaw,
though it erases cupolas and conversations
beneath its shelter,
though it leaves cities and desires
sunken in the feathers of eagles.

Freedom rolls
through a deserted world.
It's twelve in the wind
of cold truths. The help,
who's cleared the table and prepared the grapes,
on a plate offers us the voice of bells.

Who can be harmed by wind's perfection?
Hard to ask
with words that feel more shame than love
and cover their nakedness avoiding our gaze.

Difficult violets,
if what yesterday had doesn't search for tomorrow.

From *Eyestrain*

Hometown

To Regina and Miguel

By keeping my eyes wide open
in strange cities,
I can see now what you're saying,
and without shutting them
I understand your nakedness,
even though I know it
only belongs to us with eyes closed.
It must be because I'm part of your light
and darkness,
and I shift from sierras to plazas
with the same silence as your trees.

Light isn't immortal, but no one's ever lived
more than light, more than the skies
I learned to watch beneath your nights
of songs barefoot over broken glass,
city of nights revealed
in the wounded steps of my imagination,
beautiful city bearing
a cypress in the music of a piano
like I bear roses in my cold glance.

One evening when you left me behind,
I ran to look in your bag and found
two handkerchiefs of water, two cinches of bird,
a crimson thread on black walls
and clear skies,
sunglasses to watch the moon
of lost towers,
and a worn-out wallet
to fold bills and love letters,
bell towers and rooftops.

From a clean, distant rain
to the north of North,

I call you on the phone.
A familiar voice
answers, says the house's shadows
are blooming,
it's sunny, a good day
on old bridges, the halls
of the University,
the wildlife of bars with a view,
Vital Statistics and its doubts.

Decent, indispensable
like a local library,
you tremble in your traveler's coat
like a passport not wanting to get lost,
city, snowy heat,
pure impure contrast.

You're here because you seek me out
in the unstitched light of your evenings,
and not shutting my eyes
I open my luggage upon each return,
my collections of getaways,
running around the world
until a mirror returns them
to a child's height.

There are memories and trees fated to grow
with the wood shavings
of a colored pencil.

One Language

One Monarch, one Empire and one Sword
       Hernando de Acuña

I hear a voice, they're calling me by name.
I remember the map of oceans and worlds
drawn on my schoolyard,
one puddle, one empire and one sword
during the poor national autumns,
getting ruined with the rain
until it felt like earth.

I hear being said light, tree, plains
tinted by the sky
of an evening handed down with songs
in the language of Rome,
composed and decomposed,
grown in Spanish,
like children dressed in uniform
searching for two lips
so they can feel their bodies.

Language, as they explained to us,
left the world for another,
and returned with voices of legend.
I hear the flight of the condor in its syllables.
The wind blows, gathers
names and oblivion,
won't respect kilometer's sharp edge.

Born of its deaths and distances
it made out the cardinal points,
understood the buzz
of plazas used by people,
came across the violet of a far-off corner
so I might live

on the streets of Borges and Neruda
between Machado and Juan Ramón Jimenez.

The rain, not cutting
but rusting the edges of a sword,
also fell on the past,
like learning to talk
on forest leaves.
I hear a voice,
remember those school maps.

More constant than hate or greed,
mightier than bitterness or prison,
more heroic than an army's dream,
suppler than the sea
are words.

First Verses

I'm talking about those genuinely broken years.
The unpredictable wind blew round the world
through forests and hunters.
But just like forests are anywhere
there's a doubt, murmur or silence,
and hunters are always chasing the hunted,
the wind turned up and vanished
genuinely gray in any kind of helplessness.

Like in the blue-eyed man
gazing at a recently bombed city.
The corner where a child waits for a handout.
The impossible shower of a Saturday girl
opening the window to say good-bye to her john.
The shoulders of that boy passed through
by the world's wind.
It carries everything off,
everything except the hunter,

and compassion, a silenced shadow
behind beauty, a shadow to join
newer poems with my first verses.

New York

The empty bottle looks like my soul.
      José Manuel Caballero Bonald

A drunk drinks a city
until he breaks the last bottle.
It was 1929. He slept
on broken glass.

A poet writes it down. The heartbroken light
of the murdered, of those who eat the fruit
of a rootless tree
lives on in his verses.

Later there'll be a boy who reads it
and discovers the mire, the spiders
of the last trains, the corrupted dawn
of the seventies.

Still I don't know what stronger light
raised the pieces of glass toward the sky.
They're belated violets, winter emotions
on the Brooklyn Bridge.

The things of this world are thirsty.
Reality doesn't know how to keep still.
New York is my eyes. The empty bottle
can fill my soul.

The Professor

What to explain
in this maze of keys and suitcases?
Just the stations of danger
and need.

It's already four ten. The professor,
learning to live each day aloud,
recites chosen poems.
There's a quiet in the classroom
and looks cross the silence.

You need to doubt.
Suspicion offers up
a good lesson, but it's better
if no one's dispiriting,
if we each choose our doubts and keys
so when we open the suitcases
they're not empty.

Since it wouldn't be fair
to ask the May sun not to leave
the surface of something certain at the window.
Forgetting who we are,
what we should defend
so the words we say
don't smell stale
has never been the rule.
The living need trust.

We open memory with lost keys.
The poem crosses a continent,
takes a room,
unpacks its suitcase.

Always a newcomer,

doubting dogmas and affirming nothingness
the professor struggles
rather than telling the truth, to not lie,
rather than getting hopes up, to not dash them.
He'll dedicate his years
to seeking a clear reason
among shadows
and to discovering in hesitant eyes
the open luggage of a poem,
its strange commotion,
when things that happen in literature
happen in real life.

The eyes of a student
are urgent travelers. They only ask
questions like shifting sands,
questions about the next station
on a long-haul journey.

Children

Please, no noise
in the quiet of this poem
written by the hand
of one closing the door as he turns out the light.
My three children just fell asleep.
I need the silence to think of them.

Permanent colors in the pencil
of a child's tracing
once more draw
—but seriously this time—
a tree, a house, the memory
of a light glowing
with December's essence,
windows of fear
and illusions of future
beneath the workday sun.

A child is the second country we're born in.
With their early years we're forced to grow older,
and they send us back to
clockwork's realm,
to telephone calls,
roots
at the shores of time.
A child teaches us to question
earth's decisive truth
with the voice of water.
To be like reeds, flexible in love,
they don't promise
answers or rest.

Elisa, Irene, Mauro,
each with their harbor and rain,
flickering lights in the same river.

No one say anything, please,
I've just finished a poem for them.
Children grow with thorns.
I can't ever imagine
what they might say about what I've said,
what they might think of what I've thought,
what they might do with what I've done.

Market Memories

meters, liters, sharp
essence of life.
          PABLO NERUDA

They're the sung world.
A sound that gets in your eyes.

Sunlight bites
above the apple stands.
Small tributaries arrive to form
a river of questions and hands
flowing by the awnings,
greeting the flags
of the clothes rocked by wind,
skirting shoe boxes.

Like north and south,
crowds and loneliness
reach an edge where limits blur.
Eyes ask a price,
mouths startled, complain, round off
to close the deal.

Listen to the haggler's voice,
the vendor hawking oil,
cuts of fabric,
old prints.
Try on the sailor jacket,
discover the sea in this shell,
the genie in that lamp,
while the verb to exist
is a kind of fish
and the verb to be gathers
adjectives made of light the color
of fruit counters.

Come here,
murmurs of ambition,
buying and selling,
orphaned costume jewelry,
refurbished items.
Here where
city skins
and suburbs of desire embrace.

Today I find life in certain eyes
and a street blanket
with unexpected books lingering
in my imagination.
I get to me down through the Madrid edges
of El Rastro,
and I'm lost in time,
flea market,
until I slowly arrive
to San Telmo Sundays
or Friday markets in Damascus.
I've uncovered them like a creeper
of cries and oranges,
in search of the mosque
where a mystic's memory
rests in peace.

Some day the world will be perfect.
But it will be empty.

Anniversary (2004)

If our first night's
already lasted ten years,
I shouldn't be surprised
that light still holds
an uneasiness, a suit
disgraced on the hotel floor
and the awakening of a sleepless man.

Months, lives and worlds,
novels, books of poetry,
cities ablaze in my hands,
trembling heart subject to yours,
loveless trains,
boats, airplanes, they've all gone by
but nothing's done away with
the hotel night where I live
no longer myself
to call out to me with your name,
while I listen to the sea's truth
and think of the future.

It's a future I already know
the next ten years of.

Memory of Happiness
(A Beach in Rota)

To Silvia and Felipe

Life's not unfair
for being destined to change you slowly
like when I undress you.

If it weren't a poor, trembling friendship,
an intimate boarding,
time would stay silent,
at the back of the door
watching over
the truth of your skin, the evening light.

From the yard, with loud voices
our friends ask us to come down.
They want to go to town by way of the beach.

The coming waves
don't lack mysteries to place at your feet,
or sand to wipe away your steps.
My freedom bears it all,
sailing among possessive doubts.
At the sight of you walking it understands:
if you were to stay
just like you are,
delivered from the hours,
with your dark hair and your eyes,
and the faith of smooth wood
adrift in your glance,
I'd soon grow distant,
sinking deeper and deeper,
like a light grows faint on the sea
of a truth stolen by time.

Life's not unfair
though it's destined to change you slowly
like when I undress you.

Come with me to the cold of winter.
Let it all go
like a hand brushes skin,
like rain runs
down a bedroom window.
We can be happy there.
We'll surely return one day,
barefoot, embracing in the mist,
to walk along this beach
when we are wind.

My Future and Heraclitus

Long-lasting love unforeseen.
No one kisses
the same woman twice.

Prints

Snow doesn't understand, never awaits
the eyes of one watching.
Impassive, perfect it falls like a murmur
in the city of memory.

Today no one calls to me from the yard,
but I realize the voice chiding us
for going out won't keep me warm,
so I look for thick socks,
leave to walk
beside the river's poplar trees.

There's the station. There's
the trolley yellows,
the nervous bird among the reeds,
summer's fountain with its fruit immersed.

The rosebush shivers with cold.
Snow, like time,
doesn't understand the eyes of one eager to know.
It only pilfers the prints of the passerby.

No one's with me,
but on my way back I discover
other prints alongside mine,
talking softly, silently.

Like autumn they ask for
its kindling-tinted light
and scarcely greet the shiest boy,
shy Luis
who cared for the manger
where the horses ate.

Some prints end at my house.

Others go on,
winding spine-like until lost
in the city of memory.

How inhabited the abandoned places!
Just like these words written with dignity.

Translator Notes

The epigraph of part II of "To Federico, with Some Violets" is from Alan Trueblood's translation of "Lament for Ignacio Sánchez Mejías," in Federico García Lorca, *Selected Verse*. Ed. Christopher Maurer. New York: Farrar, Straus and Giroux, 1994. 272.

The epigraph of "The Night" is Charles Tomlinson's translation of "History of the Night," in Jorge Luis Borges, *Selected Poems*. Ed. Alexander Coleman. New York: Viking, 1999. 413.

The epigraph of "Market Memories" is from Mark Eisner's translation of "I Explain Some Things," in Pablo Neruda, *The Essential Neruda: Selected Poems*. San Francisco: City Lights, 2004. 65.

All other translations are the responsibility of the translators.

Lightning Source UK Ltd.
Milton Keynes UK
UKHW042107131019
351444UK00007B/133/P